WHAT I FEEL

I AM EXCITED

Beth Gottlieb

first concepts

Gareth Stevens PUBLISHING

I am excited!

It is my birthday.

I am excited!

We go to the beach.
I am excited!

Papa brings me a toy.
I am excited!

Tom comes to play.
I am excited!

Mom makes cookies.
I am excited!

We go to the pool.
I am excited!

I see a dinosaur.
I am excited!

I pet a dog.

I am excited!

I hear a good song.

I am excited!

What makes
you feel excited?

Please visit our website, www.garethstevens.com. For a free color catalog of all our high-quality books, call toll free 1-800-542-2595 or fax 1-877-542-2596.

Cataloging-in-Publication Data

Names: Gottlieb, Beth.
Title: I am excited / Beth Gottlieb.
Description: Buffalo, NY : Gareth Stevens Publishing, 2027. | Series: What I feel
Identifiers: ISBN 9781482476026 (pbk.) | ISBN 9781482476033 (library bound) | ISBN 9781482476040 (ebook)
Subjects: LCSH: Enthusiasm–Juvenile literature. | Emotions in children–Juvenile literature.
Classification: LCC BF575.E6 G68 2027 | DDC 153.1533–dc23

Published in 2027 by
Gareth Stevens Publishing
2544 Clinton Street
Buffalo, NY 14224

Designer: Deanna Lepovich
Editor: Therese Shea

Photo credits: Cover Tartila/Shutterstock.com; cover, pp. 3, 5, 7, 9, 11, 13, 15, 17, 19, 21, 23 (texture) v_kulieva/Shutterstock.com; p. 3 Sharomka/Shutterstock.com; p. 5 Evgeny Atamanenko/Shutterstock.com; p. 7 Jacob Lund/Shutterstock.com; p. 9 Prostock-studio/Shutterstock.com; p. 11 Nomad_Soul/Shutterstock.com; p. 13 Olena Yakobchuk/Shutterstock.com; p. 15 KK Tan/Shutterstock.com; p. 17 Standret/Shutterstock.com; p. 19 Dmytro Zinkevych/Shutterstock.com; p. 21 Krakenimages.com/Shutterstock.com; p. 23 LightField Studios/Shutterstock.com.

Printed in China

CPSIA compliance information: Batch #QSGS27: For further information contact Gareth Stevens at 1-800-542-2595.